31 Uses For A Zombie

by
Tim Hodge

"31 Uses for a Zombie"
written and illustrated by Tim Hodge

Published by Tim Hodge

First Edition November 2017

This is a work of fiction. Any references to any persons, historical events, or places are used fictitiously. Other names, characters, places, and events are products of the author's imagination, and any resemblance to any actual events, places, or persons living or dead (or undead), is entirely coincedental.

Printed in USA

ISBN 978-0-9858796-2-4

Follow Tim Hodge:
Tumblr & Twitter: @BaldMelonTim
Instagram: BaldMelon
Facebook: www.facebook.com/TimHodgeArt

for Abby

Introduction

This series of cartoons started out as my participation in the month-long punishment known as... Inktober.

Inktober is an art challenge started in 2009 by the incredible illustrator and sadist, Jake Parker. Jake obviously started Inktober as a torture for artists by forcing us to draw something in ink every day for the month of October. We then post our efforts on social media.

Aside from my scribblings, the internet is awash in beautiful art each October thanks to Jake.

I hope that one or two of my daily offerings for this year will bring a smile to your face.

- Tim

P.S. Anyone know how to get ink stains out of carpet?

1. Piñata

2. Staple Remover

10·3

3. Boot Scraper

4. Grape Smasher

5. Bird Cage

6. Tiki Torches

7. Cup Holder

8. Mine Sweeper

9. Cosmetic Testing

10. Tattoo Removal

11. Speed Bump

12. Racing

13. Advertising

14. Restraining Order

15. Pony Cart Rides

16. Yoga Instructor

O-17

17. Rodeo Clown

18. Caddy

19. Mailman Decoy

20. Theme Park Mascot

21. Poaching Deterrent

22. Coat Rack

23. Personal Trainer

10.24

24. Exterminator

10·25

25. Car Alarm

26. Bob Dylan Impersonator

27. Christmas Decor

28. Arcade Game

29. Batting Practice

30. Runway Model

10·31

31. Parade Balloon Handlers

Sketches

The following pages are some of my rough sketches, along with a few ideas that I didn't get around to using.

Consider this section like a DVD extra.

Enjoy! (or else)

101 USES FOR A ZOMBIE...

#49.   PIÑATA!

This is the one that started it all. It's a card I drew for my wife on her 49th birthday. (She's a big Zombie fan.)

When I drew it, I thought it was a good idea for a book, but I couldn't think of a hundred more ideas. So it sat until this year's Inktober when I dug it back up again.

THIS WAS MY WORKING
LIST ↘

- COSMETICS TESTER (MAKE-UP)
- BIRD FEEDER?
- SCRATCHING POST   YOGA
- RUNWAY MODEL   TRAINER
- MINE SWEEPER   DRUG
- DOG WALKER   MULE
- RESTRAINING ORDER ENFORCER
- THEME PARK CHARACTER / MALL
- RAKING   ELF
- CART PULLING   MINIATURE
                     GOLF OBSTACLE
- ADVERTISING (SANDWICH BOARD)
- BAGGAGE HANDLER?
- SPEED BUMP   ALLIGATOR
- VASECTOMY SURGEON → NOPE   WRESTLING

DREW THIS
ASTRONAUT GUY
ON A FAST FOOD
NAPKIN.

SPACE EXPLORATION

HEE!
HEE! ↷

GATOR
WRESTLIN'

TARGET THAT RETURNS
YOUR ARROWS

FOLLOW
UP TO
#19

DRUG MULE

BIKE RACK

EWWWWWW...

SPRINKLER

SOME RANDOM
ZOMBIE DESIGNS

BEE HIVE

RODEO CLOWN

MY WIFE CONVINCED ME THAT THE VERSION ON THE LEFT WAS FUNNIER.

MAIL MAN DECOY

I FIGURED THIS IDEA WAS BETTER WITH MORE DOGS.

What makes a good use for a Zombie? Aside from the larger question of how we will go about rebuilding society after the apocalypse, my criteria was based on the unique abilities and characteristics of the undead:

    1. Self-powered mobility.

    2. Biting.

    3. Cannot feel pain.

My best efforts relied on all three of those. One or two I still think require better set up. Like # 7. The idea there is that the hand has just sprung up from a shallow grave and the guy sets his drink into the waiting Zombie's palm. Would've been better animated, I supposed, or as a comic strip. Hopefully, the other made up for it.

Thank you for buying this collection. It was fun to make, even when I was running out of ideas.

The End

About the Author/Artist

Tim Hodge has been drawing since he was about three. That was over fifty years ago, so it's surprising that he hasn't gotten much better by now. Aside from writing about himself in the third person, he also enjoys hobbies such as playing ukulele, beekeeping, and painting.

Tim has worked in the field of animation for over 30 years. Starting out on TV commercials, he moved on to feature films, and now storyboards for various TV shows, none of which feature zombies (so far).

Tim's book of poetry "Pith & Vinegar" is available if you can find it. You can track it down on the internet, or find a big stash in his spare bedroom closet.